Let's ROCK!

Rock Painting for Kids

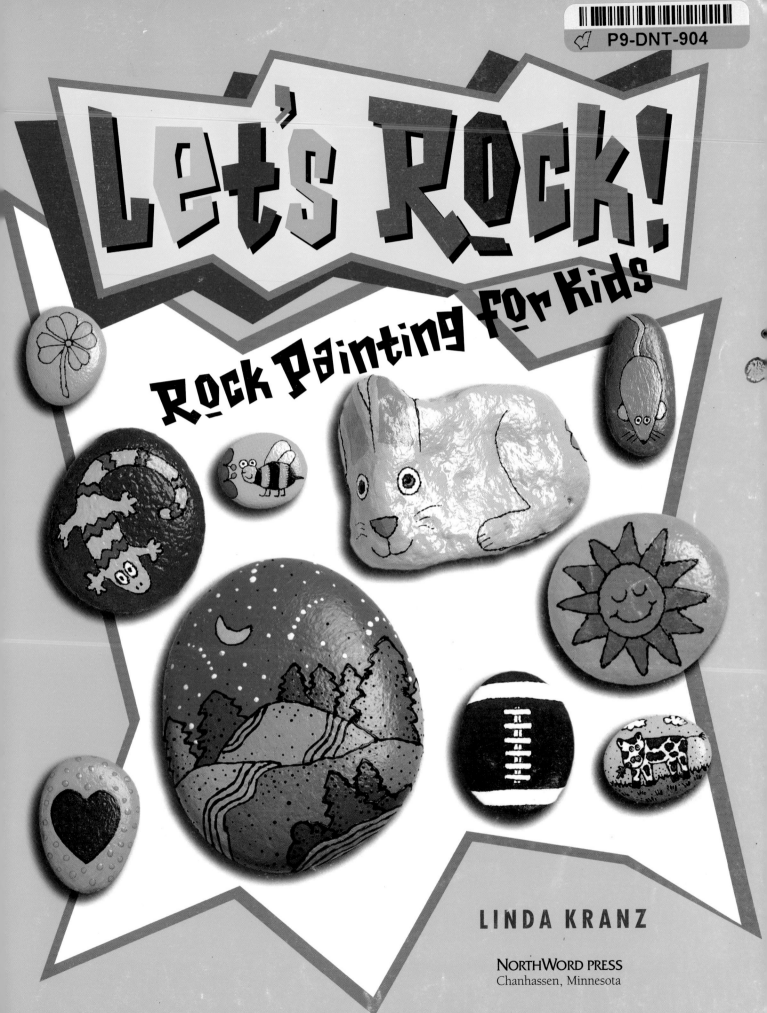

LINDA KRANZ

NORTHWORD PRESS

Chanhassen, Minnesota

The text and display type were set in Playhouse and Berkeley
Composed in the United States of America
Designed by Lois A. Rainwater
Edited by Aimee Jackson

Books for Young Readers
NorthWord Press
18705 Lake Drive East
Chanhassen, MN 55317
www.northwordpress.com

Library of Congress Cataloging-in-Publication Data

Kranz, Linda.
    Let's rock! : rock painting for kids / by Linda Kranz.
        p. cm.
    Contents: Getting started – Now let's paint – Design ideas – Gift Giving –
Now the patterns.
    ISBN 1-55971-870-6 (sc.)
    1. Stone painting—Juvenile literature. 2. Acrylic painting—Juvenile literature.
[1. Stone painting. 2. Painting. 3. Handicraft.] I. Title.

TT370.K73 2003
751.4'26—dc21   2002045510

Printed in Singapore
10 9 8 7 6 5 4 3 2 1

For Mr. Duren, my art teacher, Bitburg American High School, Bitburg, Germany. Thank you for your encouragement. You made a difference!

And for every painter: Never let anyone discourage you from expressing your creative side. Share your talents with others. With art you always leave something of yourself behind.

Table of Contents

Introduction

worth it because I received many compliments from my classmates, which made my spirits soar!

Our art classes only went up to the eleventh grade, so when I was a senior, my art teacher convinced the school staff that he had a handful of students who "needed" to continue on in art, especially their last year of school. Finally, an advanced art class was offered for seniors. Our teacher was there to guide us, yet he let us be creative. That's where my love for art began.

After high school, I found that the time I had to devote to painting seemed to shrink. I needed to find a

I began painting in high school. I took all of the required classes, but the one class I really looked forward to every day was art. Many of my friends were into band or drama, but I loved to paint. I remember painting a huge mural near the school office. It was quite an undertaking, but it was

This is one of my very first painted rocks. The rock surface was smooth and it had a small flat area that allowed the design to fit right into it. I didn't paint a base coat on the rock. I left it natural. You can look for rocks to paint that you can leave natural, too.

smaller canvas. That's when I began painting on rocks. I still have the first rock I ever painted. I enjoy seeing how my style has changed over the years.

In this book you will find the techniques I've developed over time. Patterns for all the rocks pictured throughout this book, plus a few extras, can be found on the pattern pages at the back of the book. It is wonderful to give someone a gift you have created that is one of a kind.

Be patient, have fun, and enjoy!

Linda Kranz

This is the back of a rock I painted for my husband when we were first married. On the front there is a colorful design. This was my very first attempt at painting rocks. All these years later and it still looks great!

Helpful Hints

Just for you! Wherever you see this Helpful Hints box as you read through Let's Rock!, there will be additional fun things for you to try and helpful hints that will make your rocks REALLY ROCK!

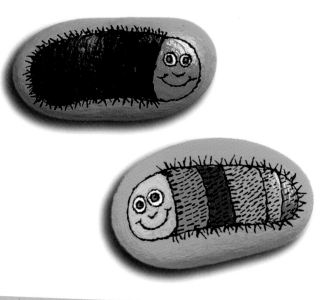

GETTING STARTED

Every child is an artist—the problem is how to remain an artist once you grow up.

—PABLO PICASSO

Getting Started

First you'll need to find your rocks. That's the fun part! You can find them in ordinary places like on the playground, in your backyard or garden, at friends' houses, in riverbeds, or if all else fails, at landscape or garden supply stores. Rocks are everywhere! Suggest that your family go on a rock finding outing some weekend. Once relatives and friends hear that you paint rocks, they will find rocks for you. Guaranteed! Friends are always sending me rocks that I can paint.

Kinds of Rocks to Look For

I found this bag of rocks at a store that sells small table-top fountains. This bundle of rocks offers a large selection of shapes and sizes. So, if you don't have time to set off on a hike to find rocks, check out the rocks at a few stores near where you live.

The rocks shown on the left have a smooth surface, and the rocks to the right have a bumpy, porous surface. Either one will work for painting the design you choose, but porous rocks will need extra base coats to cover the rock well.

Smooth, flat rocks work best. It's better if they are non-porous. Otherwise, the paint will soak in and you'll end up painting lots of coats. That takes extra time and extra paint. Bumpy rocks add interesting details, but again, it's better if they are non-porous.

You can also look for rocks that look like things, such as an animal (like this buffalo rock), or food, or a heart. Or look for rocks with interesting details and color variations. Just use your imagination! You can start a collection. Some rocks I never paint.

One thing is for sure, once you start collecting them, you will never look at rocks the same way again. Now that you are a painter of rocks, you will always be searching for that perfect rock to paint.

Here are a few of my heart rocks. Notice the rock in the top left corner. One side is clean and the other has a thin coating of mud. We were out hiking one day and I noticed a rock sticking out of the mud. One side looked like a half of a heart. I decided to pull it out and take a closer look. To my delight, the rock was shaped like a heart!

These rocks make an interesting collection. The colorful lines encircle the rocks. You can keep them in a small bowl in your room. Or if your collection grows, carefully add them to a glass jar so friends can see them when they visit you.

Stuff You Will Need

Paint

Acrylic paint works best for painting rocks—it dries fast, covers well, and if you make a mistake, you can just cover it up with more paint! You can buy a few basic colors and mix your own, or buy a large variety of colors.

These days the colors are so versatile and there is such a wide variety to choose from, I would recommend buying colors you can use right out of the tube or container: orange for a pumpkin, green for a frog, blue for the sky, yellow for a moon, or red for a heart. Then if you want to mix the colors to have lighter or darker shades, you could do that too.

Brushes

You can buy a few brushes to start out with, and then over time add to your collection. Buy a variety of different sizes. If you take care of your brushes they will last you a long, long time.

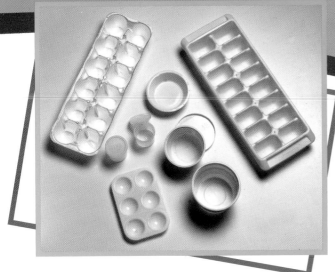

Paint Tray

You can buy a small paint tray at a craft or art supply store, or you can use a Styrofoam egg carton, an old ice-cube tray, or an empty butter dish. Whatever you use, it must be very clean, dry, and free of all oil residues, which can interfere with your acrylic paints.

Paper

You'll need paper for covering your work surface, and paper to place under your rock while you paint (plain white or brown paper, like a cut-open grocery sack, is best). Be careful not to place your freshly painted rock on newsprint as the print may rub off on the rock.

Helpful Hints

If you need to mix a color, make sure you mix enough so that you'll have some left over. It will be almost impossible to mix that exact color again. If you use paint colors directly from the tube, touch ups will be a breeze.

NOW LET'S PAINT

Imagination is more important than knowledge. Knowledge is limited. Imagination encircles the world.

—ALBERT EINSTEIN

Instructions

Prepare the Rock

1. Rinse the rock well in warm water. Try to avoid using soap if possible. Pat dry with paper towels and allow to air dry completely.

2. Lay the rock on a flat surface. Choose which side will be the "bottom" or underside of the rock, according to which side lays flat best. You will paint your design on the "top" of the rock.

3. Use a container with a lid to mix your base coat color. You will need to mix enough base coat to cover your entire rock several times, and to have enough left over to correct mistakes or pencil lines at the end. It's important that your container has an airtight lid to keep the paint from drying out.

White paint mixed with a little brown or rust makes a nice beige-colored base coat. The base coat is important because it helps the other colors adhere better to the rock.

Adding water to your paint mixture, just a little at a time, will extend your paint and make it easier to work with.

Notice that the rock on the left in the picture above has the flat side up. That rock would wobble if you touched it. If you turn that rock over and place the flat side down like the rock on the right, you'll find you have a much more stable surface on which to paint.

Use your brush to mix paint and water, and keep mixing until the colors are even and you have a thick, liquid-like texture.

4. Cover your work area with paper. Paint the top of your rock with base coat. Smooth out any bubbles or uneven paint by brushing over the rock in one direction. Allow to air dry. Repeat step several times. (Allow to air dry between each coat.)

While the rock is drying between coats, wash your brush out well with warm water (soap is not necessary) and squeeze out excess water. This will prevent your paint from clumping when you paint again. Paintbrushes can last for years if they are kept clean!

You may add a little water to the base coat as needed, but keep the lid on tight when you're not using the paint to keep it from drying out.

The thinner your base coat, the quicker it will dry! The layers of base coat do not have to be very thick at all. The purpose is to cover the rock, and give you a nice surface on which to paint your design.

The top of your rock will not need as many layers of base coat because you will be putting more paint on the top. The bottom of the rock, however, should have a nice, thick coat.

You're Ready To Paint

Now You're Ready to Paint Your Design!

1. Choose the design you wish to paint on your rock. You could pick a design from the book, or draw your own. If you choose to draw your own design, lay your rock on plain paper and draw around the rock to get the shape and size.

Then draw your design inside the rock outline.

2. Cut out your design, either your own or one from the book. Rub pencil on the back side of the cutout. Put the cutout,

You can help protect your painted rocks and make your design last longer by spraying them with a clear, protective coating. Place your finished rock on a paper towel. Spray the bottom and let it dry. Then turn it over and spray the top. You can find these products at most craft stores. Ask a grown-up to help you with this finishing touch.

3. Paint your design with your chosen color and allow to air dry completely.

4. Paint the background color on the top and sides of your rock. You may need to apply more than one coat of paint to your design or background (remember to let your rock dry between coats!).

pencil-rub side down, on the rock. Now trace the design onto the rock. Don't worry about erasing any extra pencil marks or smears as they will be covered up with paint.

You may also use graphite paper, bought at your local craft store, to trace designs onto your rock instead of using a pencil-rub.

More...

Finishing Touches

1. When your rock is completely dry, you may wish to outline your design in black (or other color) paint, or use a fine-point permanent pen.

your rock on a soft towel while you work to keep your finished design from smearing. Now use your original base coat to clean up any uneven paint lines or smudges.

2. When the top of your rock is completely dry, it's time to clean up any paint lines or smudges on the back or sides of your rock. It's a good idea to place

3. Allow your finished rock to air dry completely, and then give it to someone you love, or keep it for yourself!

Write a Message

1. If you like, you can write a message on the back of your rock. Again, trace around your rock for size and shape, but this time on a piece of lined notebook paper. Write out what you want to say on the lines within the rock shape.

3. Paint your words with black (or other color) paint, or use a fine-point permanent pen.

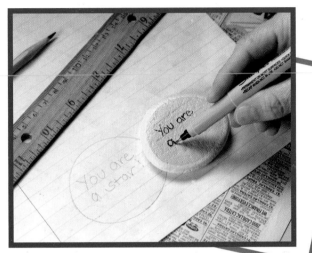

2. Position the rock next to the lines using a ruler as a guide. Then trace lines onto the rock very lightly with pencil. Now write your message on the rock lines, also very lightly in pencil.

4. Don't forget to sign your name or initials with paint or pen!

5. You may also wish to outline your message to separate where the base coat and background colors come together.

6. Finally, try to erase (using a very light hand and a very clean eraser) any visible pencil marks. Whatever you cannot erase, you can cover up with your base coat.

DESIGN IDEAS

When you can do the common things of life in an uncommon way, you will command the attention of the world.

—ANONYMOUS

Flowers

How can you see a design in a rock? Use your imagination! If a rock catches my eye, I pick it up and study the size and shape. I think about the many possibilities for painting a design on that particular rock. I love to paint flowers on rocks to give to friends or loved ones on special occasions. Unlike store-bought flowers, or flowers from the garden, a flower rock will always stay "fresh." Why not paint a flower rock for someone special? Or maybe a whole bouquet of colorful painted rock flowers? Each rock could be a different flower.

1. Paint the base coat and draw your design on the rock. Then paint your flower any color you wish. Allow the paint to dry.

2. Paint the leaves. Allow the paint to dry.

3. Choose a background color. Paint around the leaves and the flower. When your rock is completely dry, you may wish to outline your design and add more details with paint or pen.

Helpful Hints

If you have been painting for a long time, find a stopping point. Get up. Stretch. Rest your eyes. When you come back to your rock, study the design. Look at the colors. Stepping away and coming back gives you a whole new perspective. If you don't like how the colors look, you can paint over the colors you don't like. That's the nice thing about acrylic paints—they are very easy to work with.

Animals

Animals are everywhere. They share our houses with us. They live in our backyards and in our towns and cities. There are many different types of animals we can paint on rocks. Ideas are all around us. You could paint your pet or your friend's pet. You could paint a bird that lands in a tree outside your window. Or you could paint an animal that you remember seeing while you were on vacation. Look around for ideas.

1. Paint the base coat and draw the cat design on the rock.

Some rocks will remind you of an animal just by their shape. This rock was in the shape of a cat's head when I found it. Even the ears were in the perfect spot!

2. Pick the color you want to use for your cat. Paint the body of the cat. Allow the paint to dry.

3. Paint the eyes. Allow the paint to dry.

4. Paint the cat's face.

Sometimes you will find rocks in nature that will remind you of something. Notice the rock below that I found while hiking. I saw a giraffe in the outline. I showed it to several people and they couldn't "see it." Yet, when I painted the rock at the top and held it next to the natural rock, they smiled and said, " Oh, now I see it!"

5. When your rock is completely dry, use paint or pen to outline your cat and fill in the details on the face, eyes, ears, and paws.

Helpful Hints

Use a paper napkin folded in half to take excess paint off your brush. When you are painting, you don't want a bubble of paint on your brush. If you are painting a small area on your rock and a big drop of paint covers more than you had planned, you will have to let that area dry and start over. That's frustrating!

More Animals

Here are lots of fun ideas for painting different animals. Don't forget—all the patterns for these rocks are in the back of the book! Have fun and use your imagination.

Hold a rock in your hand for a while when you find it. Turn it over a few times. Use your imagination. What do you see? Some animals fit perfectly on round rocks. Sometimes you might be able to find other rocks that look just like the shape of an animal, like this duck. It looks so much like a duck, it could almost waddle!

Helpful Hints

What should you paint first? That's up to you. I paint the main design, the background, and then the black outlines.

Do you have a pet fish? A dog? A cat? A guinea pig? Take a picture of your pet and use that as your pattern guide. Or you could draw your pet on a sheet of paper. Find a rock on which you would like to paint your pet. If your photo or drawing is too big, ask a grown-up to shrink the image down on a copy machine. Once the pattern is the size of your rock, you can start to create your piece of "pet art!"

You can find different sized rocks and paint a family of crocodiles, ducks, or pigs.

How about a trip to the zoo for more ideas to paint? You can take a picture of your favorite animals, or bring a pad and pencil along and draw the animals that you want to paint.

Heart Rocks

Have you ever searched for a heart rock? They are everywhere just waiting for someone to find. I have found heart rocks in the country and in the city. You just have to train your eyes to see them. If you can't find a rock shaped like a heart, look for a rock with a nice, smooth surface on which to paint a heart. Heart rocks are wonderful to give for Valentine's Day, or any time you just want to say, "I love you."

I have a large collection of heart rocks. I have heart rocks from Canada, Germany, Italy, England, Mexico, and many states in the U.S. When friends and family find out I collect heart rocks, they find them and send them to me from all over the world! My collection keeps growing. They all hold special memories for me.

This is the only heart - shaped rock I've ever painted, and I painted it just for this book. To me, heart rocks are special and unique just the way they are, so I like to leave them in their natural state. If you find a heart rock, it is all yours and you can do with it what you like. It would be a wonderful gift to give someone either way, or to keep for yourself. What other shapes of rocks can you find to collect?

I look for heart rocks whenever I spend time outdoors with my family. But I'm also always on the lookout for other shapes of rocks, too. I keep a clipboard with lots of plain paper and a supply box filled with color pencils in my Jeep. Then if I find a rock that would be perfect for painting, I can start sketching out a few ideas. I keep the designs that I don't use for other rocks that I will paint in the future.

Sport Rocks

A ball is a perfect subject to paint for someone you know who has a favorite sport. You can search for a rock that is round. If you can't find one that's round, don't worry. Just find a rock with a flat surface and paint the shape of the ball on that rock.

Notice the two football shapes on this page. Both look like a football, but they are each on different shaped rocks. One football has a blue background so it looks like it's flying through the air for a touchdown. You could paint a ball with a green background so it looks like it is resting in green grass. There are lots of options.

You could paint a beach ball to remind a friend or loved one about a summer vacation that you took together.

You could paint a ball to give to someone for winning a big game or tournament. Or you could paint one for yourself to remember a special achievement in a game. Whether the rock is for a friend or for yourself, you could paint or write the date of the game or achievement on the back of the rock so it will never be forgotten.

Helpful Hints

I like to keep my paints in a plastic box with a lid. That way they are all in one place. And if you have little brothers or sisters who are curious, they won't be able to get into them as easily. I write down all the colors I have in my plastic paint box. Then when I go to the craft store, I bring the list along so I don't buy duplicate colors. Remember to add any new colors that you buy to your list.

Pretty Places

We all have our favorite places that we like to visit or dream about. For some it's the big city. Others may prefer a quiet field in a forest to set up camp for a few days. Some people dream about a secluded island retreat. The desert? The mountains? Where do your dreams take you?

1. Paint the base coat and draw your design on the rock. Begin to fill in the buildings with the colors of your choice.

2. Finish painting all the buildings, and then paint the sky.

This is a rock my daughter painted when she was twelve years old. She loves to watch sunsets and was inspired to paint this rock. She drew the design herself. There are several other rocks throughout this book that she also painted.

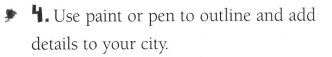

3. Paint the windows on the buildings. Paint the clouds.

4. Use paint or pen to outline and add details to your city.

Here's the same city with a night sky! Is it day or night in your city? You decide!

Let's Eat!

Sometimes when you look at different things you get all kinds of good ideas for painting on rocks. What about painting some of your favorite foods? How about a strawberry? I'll bet there are rocks out there shaped just like strawberries. Or what about a waffle? That could be a lot of fun! Warning: Looking at this page might make you hungry. But then who wants to eat a rock, right?

Yummy! My favorite! Pizza! I'll bet this one isn't too tasty though. What do you think?

Some things on these pages are real foods, the kind you eat. Then others are painted rocks. We better make sure we know which is which before we take a bite!

This fried egg looks good enough to eat! Let's see, there's over-soft, over-medium, and over-hard. I think I would call this one over-VERY-hard!

Everyone loves chocoate chip cookies!

Another favorite!
A chili dog. I painted this one because the
rock looked just like a hotdog to me. Don't you think so? Can you think of different
kinds of foods that would be fun to paint? How about an apple? Or a
banana? Maybe a hamburger,
with pickles on the side!

Helpful Hints

Throughout this book you will see rocks that are smaller than other rocks. I call these rocks "pocket rocks." They fit nicely in your pocket. You could paint one for yourself or a friend as a reminder of something. You could paint a pattern on the front. A star. A cloud. A sun. A rainbow. And on the back you could paint or write a message in your tiniest handwriting: Smile. Try. Laugh. Dream. Be Happy. Just be sure that if you carry it in your pocket, you take it out before laundry day!

Look at the orange slices on these pages. One of them is a rock, and the others are real oranges. Can you tell the difference?

Special Occasions

Holidays and special occasions come around each year. Do you have a favorite holiday? Or maybe you're looking for a gift to give someone for a special occasion. There are lots of ideas on these pages to get you started.

Add or subtract candles on the birthday cake depending on who you are painting the rock for. You can write the birthday person's name in the frosting. Choose whatever color of frosting you like!

Light your menorah this Hanukkah with rock flames that never go out! If your rock flames do not fit perfectly in your menorah, you can use removable adhesive putty (bought at your local craft store) to help hold them in place. A rock flame might also make a meaningful gift to give someone special. You could give a single rock flame, or make one to give for each night of Hanukkah.

Instead of carving a jack-o-lantern that will only last a few days, how about painting a rock jack-o-lantern that will last forever?

Here's where your imagination comes in. Tell the person you paint the present for that you've put a few things inside the box. Or you could write a card and say, "Inside this present I put a colorful rainbow, the song of a bird, a smile, a great big hug, and the sound of my laugh." I guarantee your special someone will thank you for your present! Make up a few other things that you could "put inside" the colorful box.

Even salt and pepper won't make these Easter eggs tasty, but they are fun to paint and will never "spoil"!

Here's a snowman that will never melt!

Other Fun Ideas

The ideas for painting on rocks are endless! Use your imagination. How about a smiley face? Everyone can use a smile. A rainbow? Do you see a face in the moon when it's full? Why not paint what you see? How about a star, or a constellation? A car? Your eyes or a friend's? Or maybe you'd just like to paint colorful shapes and designs on rocks. What are some other ways you can use painted rocks? You could paint several small rocks or pebbles different colors and use them for other crafts. Let your creativity run wild!

1. Paint the base coat and draw the design on the rock. Paint the earth and the ocean. Allow the paint to dry between coats.

2. Paint the black, or "space," area. Allow the paint to dry.

3. If you like, add stars around your world. Mix some white paint with a little water to thin it out. Use a tiny paint brush to add little white dots, or "stars," in the black space.

4. Use paint or pen to outline and add details to your world.

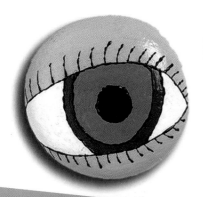

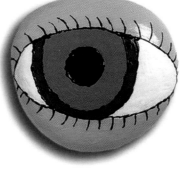

GIFT GIVING

*I dream my painting,
and then I paint my dream.*

—VINCENT VAN GOGH

Cool Gift Ideas

A handmade gift is always special. Here are some creative ways to give your painted rocks as gifts.

Good Luck

LK

You could paint several rocks to look like colorful eggs for a truly unique Easter basket. Or you could fill a basket with painted flower rocks to give as a May basket. You can choose any kind of rock to put in any kind of basket for many different gift-giving possibilities.

Choose a theme for your next birthday party and then plan ahead. You could paint a rock for each friend you invite. At each place setting you could have a rock with the name of your friend written on the back. When your party is over, your friends get to take home a piece of rock art that you've painted for them. Or you could have a rock painting party! Ask your friends to bring a rock to the party. They can choose a design from your book that they would like to paint. Painting with friends can be a great way to spend time together!

Here is a colorful way to play the game ticktacktoe. Instead of X's and O's, it's cats vs. dogs! Who do you think will win? What are some other design ideas you could use for game pieces? Once you have all your rocks painted, use a dark square of felt material for your "board" and white chalk to make the lines.

More Gifts

Here are some more gift-giving ideas. There are countless possibilities. Who do you know who might like to get a handmade gift from you? Your best friend? Your brother or sister? Your parents? Grandparents? A special teacher? I bet anyone you give your gift to will be impressed with your creativity, and will cherish it forever.

You can use a rock as a gift tag! Attach your rock to a gift bag or package with removable adhesive putty. That way, the person receiving the gift can easily remove the rock and keep it forever. What will you put in your gift box or bag? How about new paints and brushes so your friend can paint his or her own rock, too!

You could have a Halloween party and paint rock-o-lanterns! Or you could give painted rocks to your guests as party favors. A painted rock will always remind your friends of how much fun they had at your party.

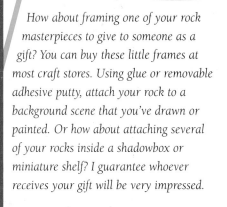

How about framing one of your rock masterpieces to give to someone as a gift? You can buy these little frames at most craft stores. Using glue or removable adhesive putty, attach your rock to a background scene that you've drawn or painted. Or how about attaching several of your rocks inside a shadowbox or miniature shelf? I guarantee whoever receives your gift will be very impressed.

To Mom

Love Sarah

NOW THE PATTERNS

These next few pages are filled with lots of patterns for you to use. You can either cut the patterns right out of the book, or you can use tracing paper to trace over the designs you want to use. If you cut out the patterns, you could store them in an envelope and tape the envelope to the inside back cover of this book. That way, all your patterns will be in one place in case you want to reuse them.

What if you find a rock that is a different size from a pattern you want to use? Just ask a grown-up to make you a larger or smaller copy using a copy machine so the pattern will fit nicely onto your rock. If you would like the design on a pattern to face the opposite direction, no problem. Just hold the pattern up to a sunny window with the pattern side facing the window (away from you). Trace the design onto the backside of the pattern. Now the design is facing the other direction!

This is a book of ideas. We all want to be creative. Once you feel comfortable, add your own touch to the rock designs in this book, or create your own new designs. You are the artist! Have fun!

I would love to see pictures of the rocks that you've painted! Please send me photos of your creations.

Linda Kranz
P.O. Box 2404
Flagstaff, AZ 86003-2404